THIS BOOK BELONGS TO

_____

All questions and answers in this book are accurate as of October 2020

GOLF RECORDS

Across

1. Since 2000 only two players have managed to win 9 PGA titles in a single season. Tiger Woods did it in 2000 but who else managed this in 2004?

3. Which American golfer hit the lowest round in history of 58 at the travelers championship in 2016?

4. Who is the oldest golfer to win a major. He was 48 years old and won when he won the 1968 PGA championships.

6. Who holds the record for the most major titles?

11. Tiger Woods holds the record for the most titles won at a single tournament being the Arnold Palmer invitational. How many times did he win it?

13. The most consecutive birdies hit in a row to win a tournament was 7. Who with the first name Kevin managed this in 2014?

16. The fastest ever round of golf was achieved by 80 golfers playing on the same course. To the nearest minute, how long did it take them?

Down

2. What Spanish golfer holds the joint record for losing the largest lead after 54 holes in 2005 (6 shot lead)?

5. Who is the second youngest golfer to win a major at 21 years and 8 months old?

7. Jack Nicklaus and Arnold Palmer hold the record for the most consecutive years with a win. How many years was this?

8. In what Asian country can you find the longest hole of golf in the world (964 yards)?

9. Who holds the record for the most tournaments won for someone in their 30s?

10. What is the largest number of golfers that there has ever been in a playoff?

12. Allenby and Sutton hold the record for the most PGA hole in ones over their careers, but how many hole in ones was it?

14. Who is the oldest golfer to win a PGA tour title? This golfer achieved this in 1965 and is a legend of the game.

15. Who is fourth on the list for the most PGA titles with the first name Ben?

"SUCCESS IN THIS GAME DEPENDS LESS ON STRENGTH OF BODY THAN STRENGTH OF MIND AND CHARACTER."
–ARNOLD PALMER

TIGER WOODS

Across
4. Tiger Woods won the 1997 Masters by 12 shots. What did he shoot on his opening nine holes of the tournament?
5. How many other golfers besides Tiger finished under par in the 2000 U.S. Open?
8. Which state was Tiger born in?
9. What is the largest winning margin in Tigers career?
11. Who is Tiger Woods' main sponsor?
12. Where did Tiger win his first title in 1996?
14. Tiger holds the PGA TOUR record for most seasons of five-plus wins. He won five or more events in how many seasons?
15. Who coached Tiger from between 1993-2004?

Down
1. Tiger has won 11 out of the 12 play offs that he's played in. Which golfer with the first name Billy beat him?
2. At what age did Tiger start playing golf?
3. Where does Tiger's mother Kutilda hail from?
6. What is Tigers real first name?
7. Who has Tiger finished runner up to the most times?
10. Where did Tiger win his first major title?
13. To the nearest 100, how many weeks has Tiger spent at number 1?

"A GOOD GOLFER HAS THE DETERMINATION TO WIN AND THE PATIENCE TO WAIT FOR THE BREAKS."
—GARY PLAYER

AUGUSTA MASTERS

Across
4. How many times has Jack Nicklaus won the masters?
5. Only three players have won the Masters in consecutive years: Jack Nicklaus, Tiger Woods and who?
7. Which Canadian won the masters in 2003?
9. Across the history of the masters, which hole has proven to be the hardest, based on the average score above par?
10. Gary Player was the first non-American to win the masters. Who was the second?
13. The fourth hole at Augusta is now called Flowering Crabapple. What was its original name?
14. In 2017 only 3 Americans finished in the top 10. Who was the leading American that year?
15. Who is the first non-American player to win the masters in 1961?

Down
1. Guan Tianlang became the youngest player to make the cut at the Masters in 2013. How old was he?
2. When Ian Woosnam snatched the masters title in 1991, who was the leading amateur that year?
3. America boasts the record for the most masters wins, but South Africa and what country are joint second on the list?
6. Tiger Woods's chip-in at the par three 16th, considered the best shot in history by some, propelled him to victory in 2005. But who did he beat in a play-off?
8. Who was a surprise winner at the 2016 masters?
11. Greg Norman is considered to be the best player never to have won the masters. How many times did he finish in the top 3?
12. Who won the masters in 2017?

"GOLF IS A COMPROMISE BETWEEN WHAT YOUR EGO WANTS YOU TO DO, WHAT EXPERIENCE TELLS YOU TO DO, AND WHAT YOUR NERVES LET YOU DO."
—BRUCE CRAMPTON

GENERAL KNOWLEDGE

Across
6. Which course has been used more often than any other for The Open Championship? (29 times)
8. Who became the first European player to score what is now the maximum of five points in a single Ryder Cup in 2018?
10. What is the maximum number of minutes that you are allowed to look for a lost ball for?
13. By what name is the trophy presented to the winner of The Open Championship most commonly known?
15. Lee Westwood and what other golfer are the only two players that have been ranked number one without winning a major?

Down
1. Which golfer recorded the most points for USA in the 2019 Ryder Cup?
2. Who was top of the golf world rankings prior to lockdown?
3. Who won his only Open Championship at Royal St Georges, Sandwich in 1985?
4. Royal St George's Golf Club is based in which English town that shares its name with a popular lunchtime food?
5. The 11th, 12th and 13th holes at Augusta National are collectively known by what nickname?
7. Which Swedish golfer, who retired in 2008 with 90 international titles, is widely regarded as the best ever female player?
9. Name the only non-American player to win a major in 2019?
11. Who stunned the golf world by winning the 2003 PGA Championship despite being ranked No. 169th in the world at the time?
12. Under the rules of golf, what's the maximum number of clubs allowed in a player's golf bag during a round?
14. Which golf term is defined as the "area of grass surrounding the putting surface"?

"ACHIEVEMENTS ON THE GOLF COURSE ARE NOT WHAT MATTERS, DECENCY AND HONESTY ARE WHAT MATTER."
—TIGER WOODS

RYDER CUP

Across
2. Sergio Garcia needed three points in Paris to become Europe's all-time highest scorer in Ryder Cups. Who previously held that record?
5. Four players failed to score a point for Europe at Hazeltine; Lee Westwood, Danny Willett, Matt Fitzpatrick and who else?
7. Which player made his debut as a 19-year-old, making him the youngest player in Ryder Cup history?
8. Before Davis Love III guided team USA to victory in 2016, who was the only other winning American captain of this century?
10. Which European pair have won more points playing together than any other? Olazabal and _____
11. Who was the only European player to finish unbeaten at Hazeltine?
14. Which country played host to the 2006 Ryder Cup?
15. Thomas Bjorn captained Europe at Le Golf National, but how many times did he represent Europe as a player?

Down
1. Its 25 years since team USA last won on European soil. Who captained the Americans to victory?
3. Who was the European Captain in the 1995 Ryder Cup matches?
4. Whose figure adorns the Ryder Cup?
6. Where was the 2002 Ryder Cup held?
9. Who secured the winning point for team USA in their 17-11 victory at Hazeltine?
10. Who was Jamie Donaldson playing against when he secured the winning point for Europe at Gleneagles in 2014?
12. Out of the eight Ryder Cups that Tiger Woods has played, how many has he won?
13. Who sank the winning putt to secure the Cup during the 'Miracle at the Medinah'?

"The more I work and practice, the luckier I seem to get."
–Gary Player

GUESS THE PLAYER

Across
2. This golfer was born in 1929 and was known as the 'king' of golf. He is a 7-time major winner, and 4-time winner at Augusta.
5. This golfer was born in 1931 and was one of the most prolific tournament winners from the 50s-70s. He had the nickname Buffalo Bill.
7. This Fijian golfer was the leading PGA tour money winner in 2003, 2004 and 2008.
10. This golfer has finished runner up in all four majors. He famously got an albatross at the 2012 masters where he would end up winning the tournament.
12. This golfer born in 1947 was the first player to shoot a 63 at the 1973 US open, which he went on to win. He also won the 1976 open championships.
13. This player was born in 1984 and won the 2016 US open. He is a famous for his long drive.
15. This golfer was ranked world number one from mid-May to August in 2014 and has won a total of 31 titles.

Down:
1. This 29-year-old English golfer is famous for his long hair. He has two runners up finishes at majors.
3. This German golfer is a two-time masters champion and is one of five who have won tournaments on all six continents where golf is played.
4. 'The Big Easy' as this golfer was known is a former world number 1 and has won four majors. He stands at 6 foot 3.
6. This English golfer is known as 'Beef'.
8. This English golfer was born in 1994. He won the 2013 US amateurs, and his first of 5 professional wins came at the 2015 British open.
9. This American golfer nicknamed the scientist shook the golf world this year by adding 30 pounds to his frame.
11. This golfer has earned himself the nickname 'captain America' because of his success at the Ryder Cup.
14. This American golfer won the 2018 Players championships. He is 6 foot 2 and has 7 professional wins.

"GOLF IS A SCIENCE, THE STUDY OF A LIFETIME, IN WHICH YOU CAN EXHAUST YOURSELF BUT NEVER YOUR SUBJECT."
–DAVID FORGAN

RORY MCILROY

Across
2. How many times has McIlroy won the FedEx Cup?
5. How old was McIlroy when he won his first PGA Tour event?
8. How many Major Championships has McIlroy won?
9. Mcilroy shot a career-low round of 61 to help him win which 2019 open tournament?
10. Where did McIlroy win his first pro event?
11. Where does Mcilroy rank amongst Europeans for most PGA titles won?
13. How many PGA Tour wins does he have?
15. Who was McIlroy's first Ryder Cup partner?
16. Who did McIlroy beat with the first name Ryan in a play-off at the 2016 Tour Championship to win his first FedExCup?

Down
1. McIlroy was unable to defend The Open Championship in 2015 after injuring his ankle after playing what sport?
3. Which professional tennis player was Mcilroy engaged to in 2013?
4. How many Ryder Cup appearances has McIlroy made?
6. Rory finished in 2nd place at the 2018 British Open Championship. Which Italian golfer ended up finishing two-strokes ahead of Rory to win the tournament?
7. Who did McIlroy beat in a playoff to win his latest PGA Tour title at the WGC-HSBC Champions in November 2019?
12. McIlroy just needs to win the Masters to complete golf's Grand Slam. What is his best result at Augusta National?
14. In 2011, McIlroy was criticised by Phil Mickelson for skipping which high-profile championship?

"A GOOD PLAYER WHO IS A GREAT PUTTER IS A MATCH FOR ANY GOLFER. A GREAT HITTER WHO CANNOT PUTT IS A MATCH FOR NO ONE."
–BEN SAYERS

MAJORS WINNERS

Across
2. Willie Anderson was the first golfer to win four US Opens (1901, 1903, 1904 and 1905). Who was the next golfer to win four US opens?
8. Three golfers won three consecutive British Opens in the 1800s. Who was the only golfer to win three consecutive British Open in the 1900s?
9. Which of the majors only had a one-year break due to world war two?
11. Who won the first open championships after the second world war in 1946?
12. What South Korean golfer won the 2009 PGA championships?
14. What South African golfer won his second major at the 2004 US open?
15. What Australian golfer won the 2015 PGA championships?

Down
1. Which Zimbabwean golfer won his third and final major at the 1995 PGA championships?
3. What South African won the 2008 masters?
4. Who was the first Australian born golfer to win one of the four majors?
5. This Argentinian golfer known as 'El Pato' won both the 2007 US open and the 2009 masters.
6. Which American golfer won his first major at the 2019 US open?
7. Which American won his second and final major at the 1995 Masters?
10. Who was the winner of the 2016 open championships?
13. Who won the 2019 Open Championships?

"EVERYBODY CAN SEE THAT MY SWING IS HOMEGROWN. THAT MEANS EVERYBODY HAS A CHANCE TO DO IT."
—BUBBA WATSON

GENERAL KNOWLEDGE 2

Across
1. In 1967 which golfer made the first televised hole in one?
3. Which country is sixth on the list for most golf courses with a total of 637?
4. Which golfer is known as the Walrus?
5. Which four letter word refers to a movement disorder known to interfere with putting?
8. The Ryder Cup is named after English businessman Samuel Ryder who made most of his money selling what?
10. Which common slang term is often used for the clubhouse (or even sometimes a pub close to the course)?
13. Which trophy is played for by women golfers from the United States in competition with Britain and Ireland?
14. Which country is third on the list for most golf courses with a total of 2295?
15. Who was involved with John Daley in the 1995 British Open play-off?

Down
2. Who is 'The Golden Bear'?
6. Great Britain and what other nation opposed the US in the Ryder cup between 1973-77?
7. Over how many holes is the British Open Golf tournament contested?
9. At the 2016 Summer Olympics in Rio de Janeiro, which golfer won gold in the men's individual tournament?
11. Who did Nick Faldo sensationally beat to win his third Masters?
12. In 1996 what former world number one tennis player (and coach of Andy Murray) made his debut at the Czech Open?

"THE GAME HAS SUCH A HOLD ON GOLFERS BECAUSE THEY COMPETE NOT ONLY AGAINST AN OPPONENT, BUT ALSO AGAINST THE COURSE, AGAINST PAR, AND MOST SURELY AGAINST THEMSELVES."
–ARNOLD PALMER

PHIL MICKELSON

Across
5. How many victories does Mickelson have in all four majors combined?
6. Which of the majors has Mickelson won on the most occasions?
9. What is Mickelson's biggest ever margin of victory?
10. Mickelson was the third left hander to win a major. Who was the second?
11. How many times has Phil finished runner-up in The Open Championship?
12. Which equipment brand did he switch to in 2004?
13. When Phil won at Augusta in 2006, he was paired with which former champion in the final round?
15. To the nearest 100, how many weeks has Phil spent in the top 10?

Down
1. How many Ryder Cups has Mickelson won?
2. Phil left which equipment manufacturer in 2004?
3. Phil birdied the 18th to win the Masters in 2004 - but who finished second?
4. Mickelson won his third masters in 2010. Which British golfer came second in this tournament?
7. Which university did Phil graduate from?
8. What was the last major that Mickelson won?
14. How many Ryder Cup appearances has Mickelson made?

"GOLF GIVES YOU AN INSIGHT INTO HUMAN NATURE, YOUR OWN AS WELL AS YOUR OPPONENT'S."

−GRANTLAND RICE

GENERAL KNOWLEDGE 3

Across
3. What is the governing body for golf in the USA?
4. Which famous golf player is nicknamed "Lefty"?
9. What is it called if you get four shots under par on a single hole?
10. Female golfer and career grand slam winner, Juli Inkster hails from which nation?
12. Coby Orr is the youngest person to ever make a hole in one. He achieved this in 1975 but how old was he?
13. Where was the game of golf invented?
14. Which American golfer was nicknamed "The Joplin Ghost"?
15. What language is the word caddy derived from?

Down
1. In a game of golf, a low hook short, which does not go very far, is known as?
2. An unbelievable 375-foot putt was made in 2001 at St Andrews for the longest put ever. Who made this putt?
5. Bobby Locke was a popular golf player. Which nation did he come from?
6. Which golfer was the winner of 2018 U.S. Open Champion?
7. What is it called when you strike the ground before making contact with the ball?
8. In golf, which other word refers to the terminology "a hole-in-one"?
11. This is a bad shot which by mutual agreement between playing partners is cancelled and replayed.

"REVERSE EVERY NATURAL INSTINCT AND DO THE OPPOSITE OF WHAT YOU ARE INCLINED TO DO, AND YOU WILL PROBABLY COME VERY CLOSE TO HAVING A PERFECT GOLF SWING."
–BEN HOGAN

FINISH THE GOLF COURSE

These are based on the top 100 golf courses according to Golfdigest

Across
3. Winged _____. This course is in New York and was founded in 1923. It is ranked number 14.
5. Cypress _____ club. This is a private golf course in California. It is well known for its dramatic holes and is ranked 4.
6. _____ Dornoch. This club is in Scotland and is ranked number 5.
7. Pine _____. This course can be found in Southern New Jersey and is ranked number 3.
9. Royal Birk_____ (one word). This golf course is used for the Open Championships. It is ranked number 35.
11. _____oustie (one word). This golf course is used for the open championships. It is ranked number 26.
13. Muir_____ (one word). This golf course is used for the Open Championships. It is ranked number 9.
14. Morfon_____ (one word). This golf course was designed in 1927 and can be found in Paris. It is ranked number 7.
15. Shinnecock _____. This is a links course that is in New York. It is ranked number 7.

Down
1. Royal county _____. This is a golf club in Northern Ireland, located in Newcastle, County Down. It is ranked number 1.
2. Tara _____. This course can be found in New Zealand and is ranked number 2.
4. Royal Mel_____ (one word). This course can be found in black rock Australia and is ranked number 23.
8. The old course at St _____. This course is considered to be the oldest golf course in the world and is known as the 'home of golf'. It is ranked number 6.
10. Oak_____ (one word). This course is located in Pennsylvania and was created in 1903. It is ranked number 11.
11. South _____ owners club. This course has only been open since 2013 and can be found in South Korea. It is ranked number 9.
12. Royal Port_____ (one word). This golf course is used for the Open Championships. It is ranked number 27.

"IT'S ABOUT HITTING THE BALL IN THE CENTRE OF THE CLUB FACE AND HITTING IT HARD."
–BUBBA WATSON

JACK NICKLAUS

Across

2. Who beat Jack in the 1964 Open at St. Andrews?
4. How many times did Nicklaus win the British open?
7. What message did Jack's son write him on the back of his scorecard as he approached the green on the final day of the 1980 US open. Jacks _____.
8. Nicklaus was the first to win a specific major tournament twice in a row. Which major was it?
10. Nicklaus has the third highest total of wins on the PGA tour, with how many?
11. In the final round of the 1986 Masters, Nicklaus shot a 65 to come from four shots back to win. What did he shoot on the back nine to finish off the victory?
12. How many times was Nicklaus a runner-up at The Open Championships?
13. As an amateur in 1960, Nicklaus finished runner-up to Arnold Palmer in the U.S. Open. Still an amateur in 1961, what place did he finish as Gene Littler won the same title?
15. Where did Nicklaus attend college?

Down

1. Who introduced Nicklaus to golf?
3. How old was Nicklaus when he started playing golf?
5. Who beat Jack in the 1960 US Open at Cherry Hills?
6. Who beat Jack in the 1964 PGA at Columbus?
9. Who beat Jack in the 1968 US Open at Oak Hill?
14. How many major titles did Nicklaus win in his second professional year?

"FORGET YOUR OPPONENTS; ALWAYS PLAY AGAINST PAR."
—SAM SNEAD

BRITISH GOLFERS

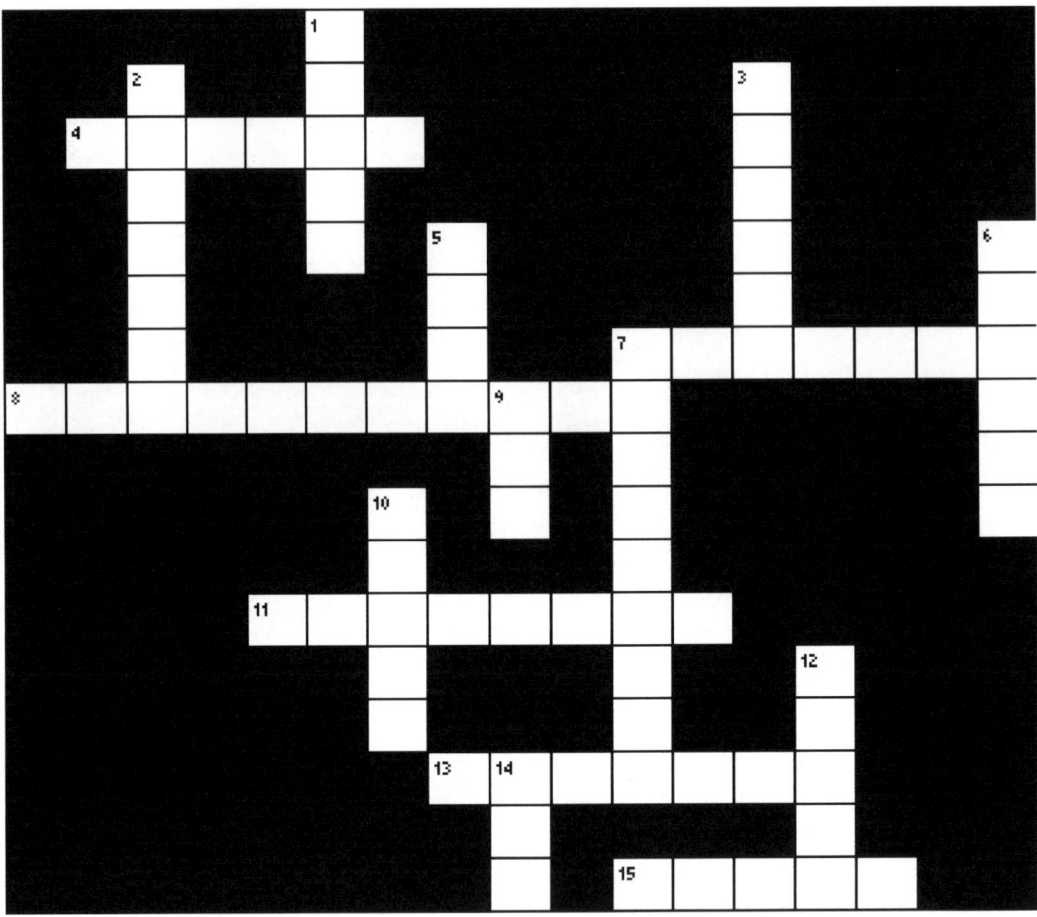

Across
4. This golfer was born in 1991. He has won five times on the European Tour including three Rolex Series events.
7. What is Ian Poulters nickname?
8. This golfer was born in 1963 and has won the most European tour events (31). His highest ranking was number 2.
11. Nick Faldo has worked for BBC sport since 2012. Which broadcasting company did he work for since 2006 before then?
13. This golfer turned pro in 1995 and reached a career high ranking of 5. He finished second in the open championship in 2008.
15. How many times did Nick Faldo win the Open Championships?

Down
1. Lee Westwood became the world number 1 golfer in 2010. Who did he replace as number 1 at the time?
2. This golfer was born 1944. He was Ryder cup captain from 1983-89 and won two majors.
3. This golfer was born in 1931 and played in 8 Ryder cups. He won 20 pro tournaments and represented England at the Olympics 10 times.
5. How many times did Montgomerie come runner up in majors?
6. This golfer was the first Englishman to be named PGA player of the year, and European tour golfer of the year. He was born in 1977.
7. This player with the first name Eddie won his first European tour event in Qatar in 2018. He has since gone on to win 3 professional events.
9. Where were the Olympics held when Rose won in 2016?
10. This golfer was born in 1977 and achieved a career high ranking of number 3 in 2009. He finished third in the Open Championships in 2010.
12. How many second-place finishes has Westwood had at majors?
14. What is Justin Rose's highest world ranking?

"A PERFECTLY STRAIGHT SHOT WITH A BIG CLUB IS A FLUKE."
–JACK NICKLAUS

JORDAN SPIETH

Across
3. What was special about Spieth's poor 2018 season?
5. Spieth finished in 2nd place at the 2015 PGA Championship. Who won the tournament?
6. Which school did Spieth play for in college?
7. At what course did Spieth win the 2015 U.S. Open? It is a two-word course with the second word being bay.
9. What sport was Jordan Spieth's first love?
10. At the 2016 masters, how big was Spieth's lead coming into the back 9?
11. What is Spieth's nickname?
12. How many majors has Spieth won?
13. Which duo did Spieth beat by one stroke to win the U.S. Open in June 2015? Oosthuizen and _____?
15. Spieth finished in 2nd place at the 2014 Masters. Who won the tournament?

Down
1. What was the first Major Championship that Spieth won in 2015?
2. Jordan Spieth is the second youngest player to earn a Master's green jacket, next to _____.
4. Which masters has Spieth never won?
8. What is Spieth's lowest score in a round on the PGA Tour?
14. When Spieth collapsed at the 2016 Masters, how many shots did he need on the par 3 twelfth?

"NEVER CONCEDE THE PUTT THAT BEATS YOU."
—HARRY VARDON

ANSWERS

GOLF RECORDS

TIGER WOODS

AUGUSTA MASTERS

```
            F           M
            O       S I X
            U       C
  S         R       K
F A L D O   W E I R   T E N T H
  P   I   W   E       L
  A   M   I   E       S
  I B A L L E S T E R O S
  N   R   L   I   N   O
      C   L   X       N
      O   E       G
          T   T H E P A L M
                  R
              K U C H A R
                  I
              P L A Y E R
```

GENERAL KNOWLEDGE

RYDER CUP

GUESS THE PLAYER

RORY MCILROY

MAJORS WINNERS

GENERAL KNOWLEDGE 2

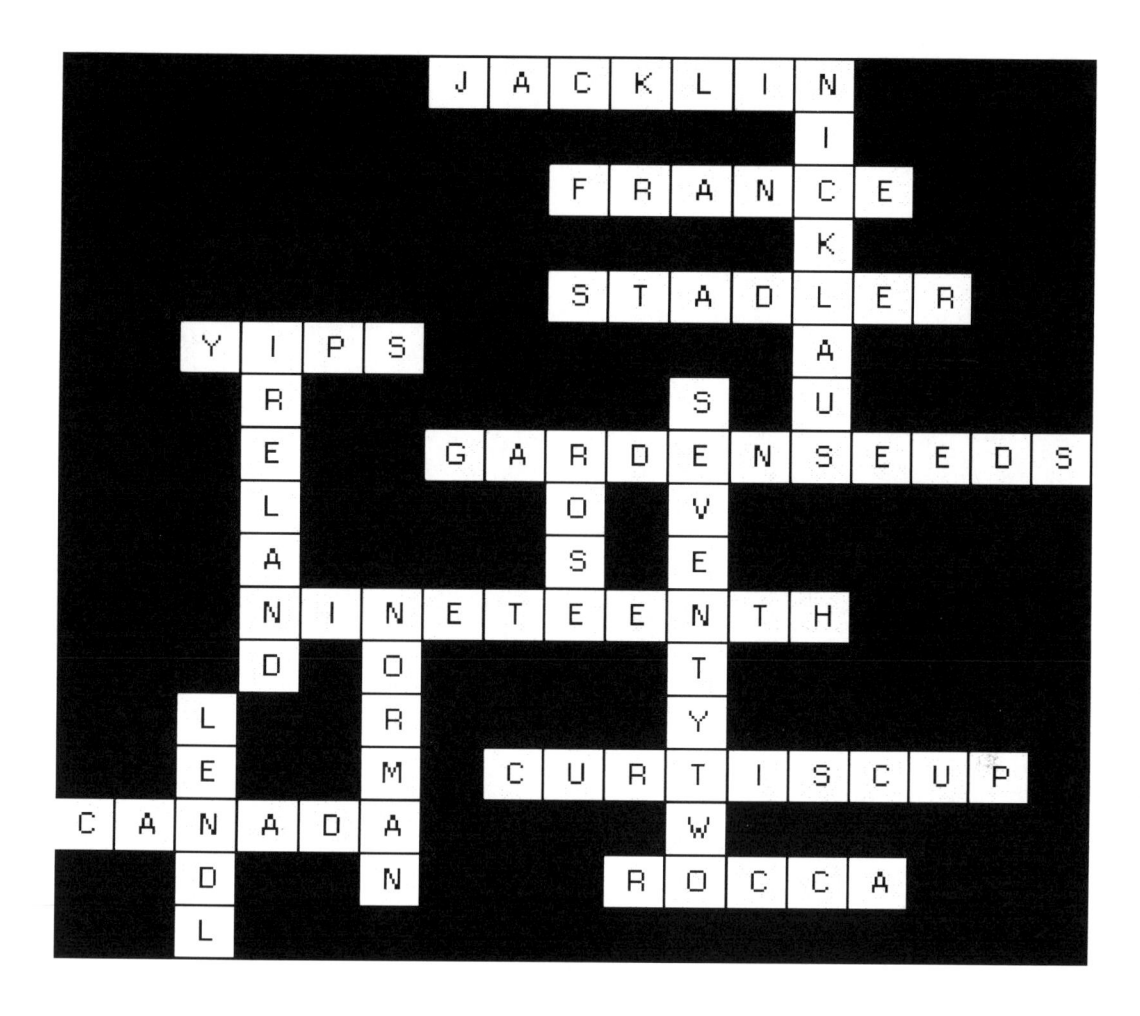

PHIL MICKELSON

GENERAL KNOWLEDGE 3

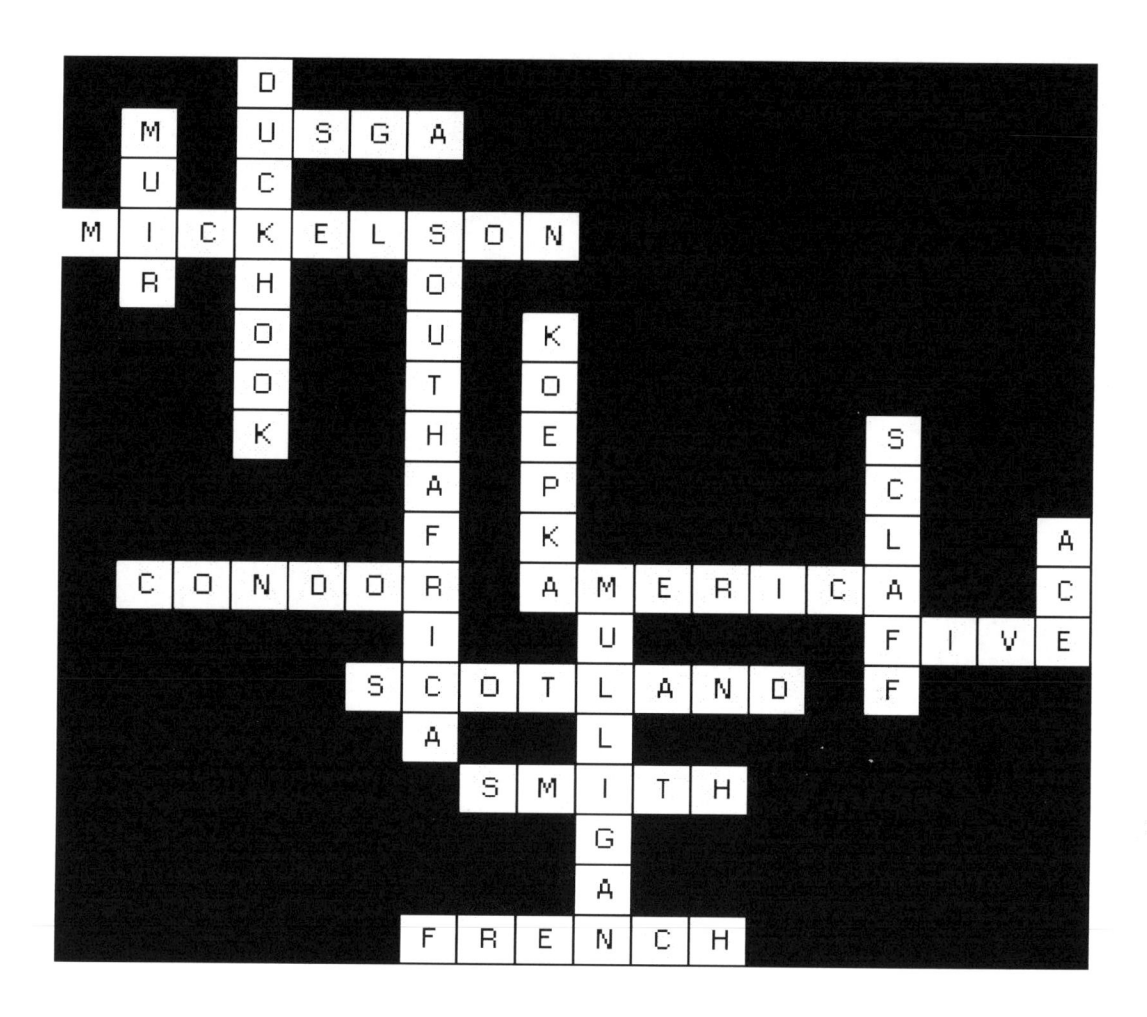

GOLF COURSES

JACK NICKLAUS

BRITISH GOLFERS

JORDAN SPIETH

Printed in Great Britain
by Amazon